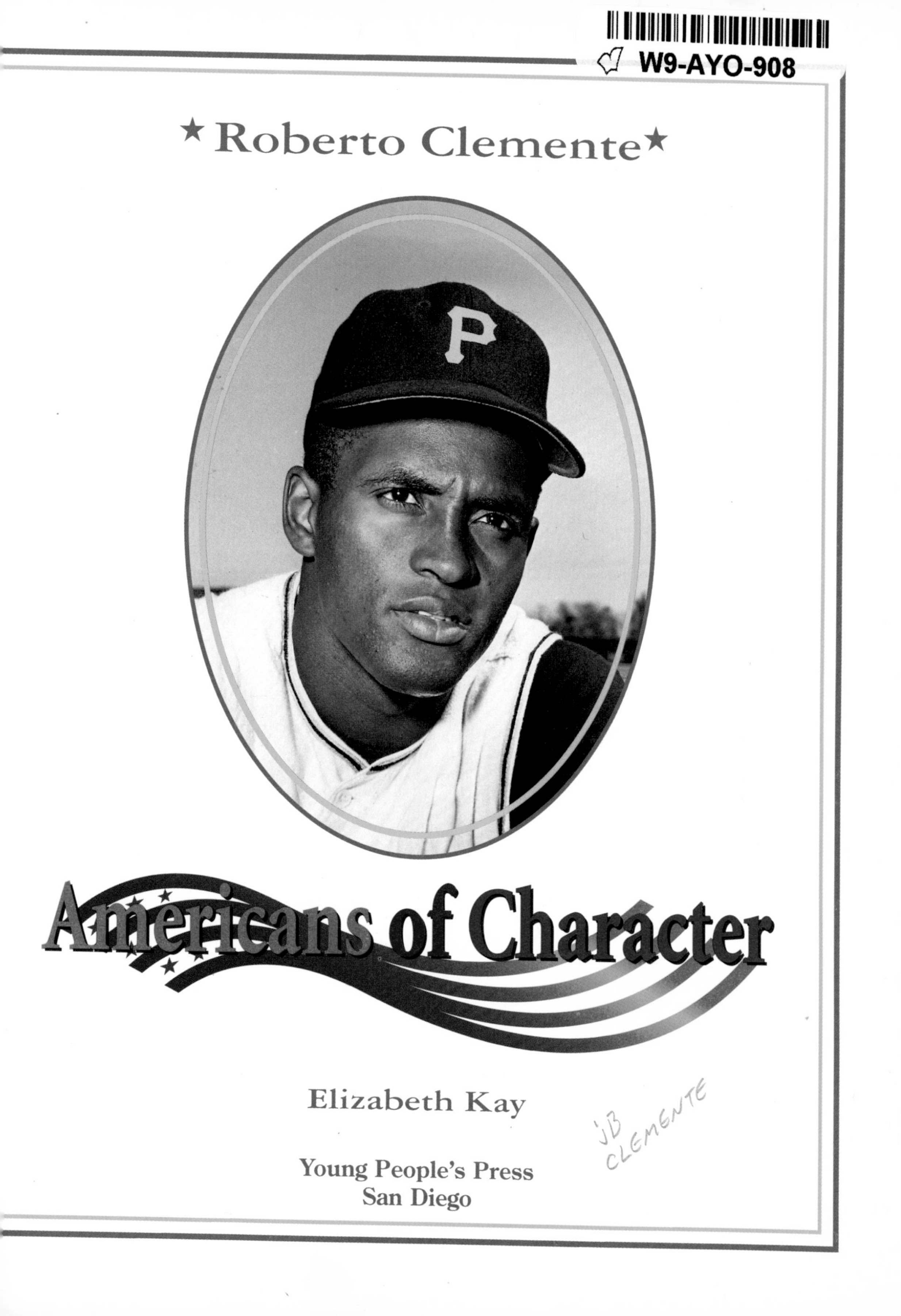

★Roberto Clemente★

Americans of Character

Elizabeth Kay

Young People's Press
San Diego

About the *"Six Pillars of Character"*

Each section of this book includes a drawing of a pillar. Above each pillar is a word. These words—six in all—name the most important traits that a person of good character has. Together, these words are known as the *"Six Pillars of Character."* On pages 22 – 27 you will be exploring what these pillars mean.

Cover photo, UPI/Bettmann.

Published in the United States of America.

2 3 4 5 6 7 8 9 - 02 01 00 99 98 97

ISBN 1-57279-063-6

Table of Contents

1 SPORTS CENTER

Roberto Clemente grew up in Puerto Rico. More than anything else, he loved to play baseball. He played it wherever and whenever he could. He played baseball in the streets, in yards, and in sandlots. There wasn't a good facility for him and other kids to use.

When Roberto became a famous baseball star, he wanted to build a Sports Center near his home town, Carolina. There, all kids could practice sports for free. He said about this dream: **"It is the biggest ambition of my life. . . It will be open to everybody, no matter who they are. . . Baseball is just something that gave me a chance to do this."**

CARING

Roberto Clemente shared his good fortune with others.

2 WORLD SERIES

Dreaming of being a baseball star is one thing, but actually becoming one is quite another! Roberto had the dream, and he also had the drive. Sure, there were times when Roberto wanted to quit. Yet his desire to do his best was always there. He played for years on a losing team, daily trying to improve himself. Greatness did not come to him overnight.

Eventually, though, all of Roberto's work, pain, and drill paid off. The Pittsburgh Pirates made it to two World Series. Roberto got a hit in every game!

Roberto Clemente always did his best.

RESPONSIBILITY

3 BASES FOR A TRIPLE

Hitting singles or doubles in the Major Leagues is quite an accomplishment. Hitting a triple is just plain amazing! It takes a combination of explosive hitting and daring baserunning. Yet Roberto Clemente became famous for hitting triples. His strength and speed were legendary. He gained these things through hard work.

Clemente was speedy, but sometimes he had to slide to reach third base safely.

RESPONSIBILITY

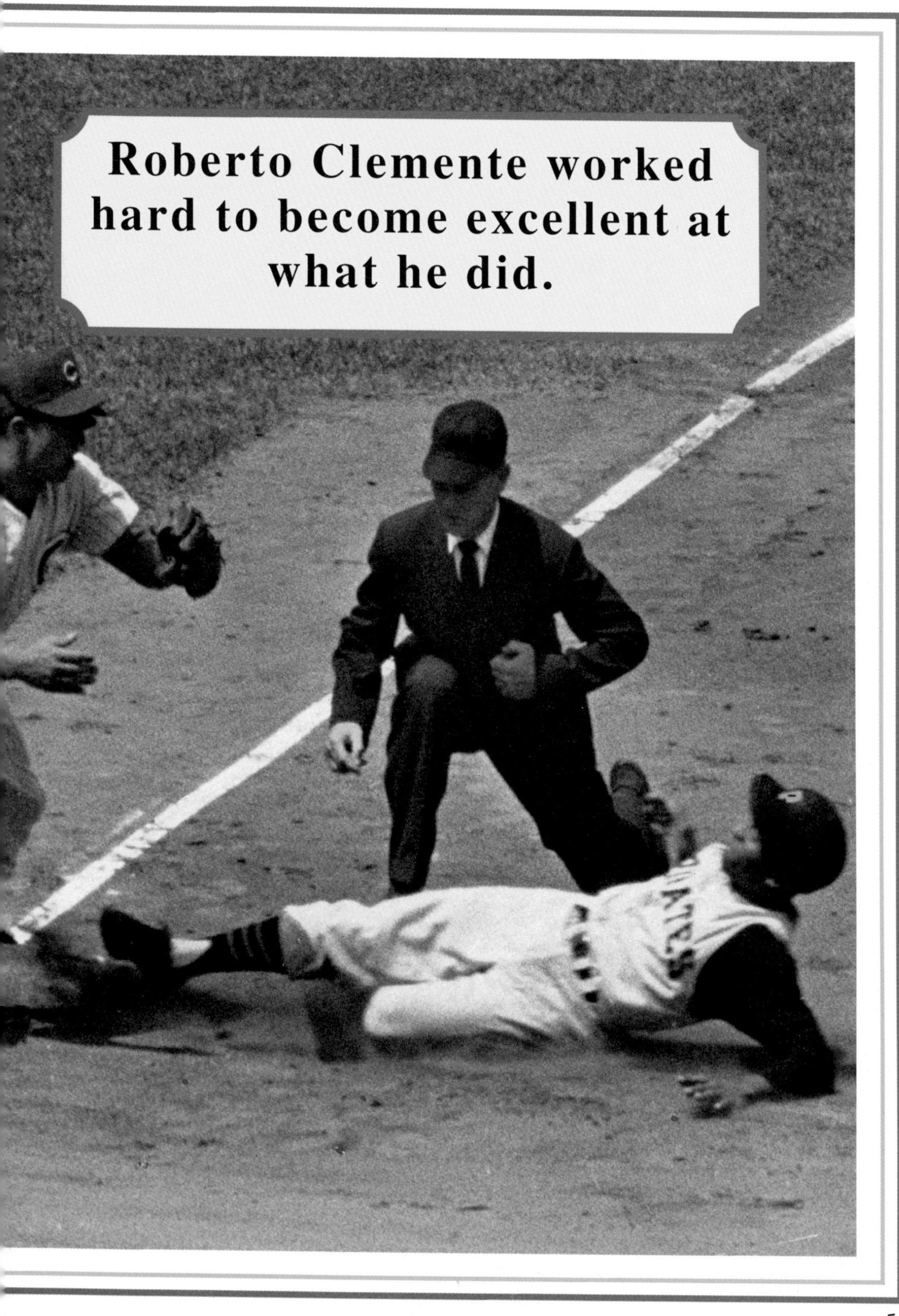
Roberto Clemente worked hard to become excellent at what he did.

4 NATIONAL LEAGUE BATTING TITLES

Roberto earned many awards in the 18 years he played Major League baseball. He was rightfully proud of winning four batting titles. But the award he had his heart set on was Most Valuable Player. In 1960, he got so few votes for MVP that his teammates teased him and called him "No Votes." This made him all the more determined to win the MVP.

In 1966, he did!

Roberto Clemente was committed to always improving and disciplined about doing it.

The MVP award (right) meant more to Roberto than any other award.

TRUSTWORTHINESS

5 DAYS IN THE HOSPITAL

Roberto hurt himself many times playing ball. Sometimes he ran so hard that he crashed. Sometimes he threw so hard that he hurt his arm. One time the Pirates were playing in Chicago when Roberto crashed into the wall while he was going for a fly ball. This time he ended up in the hospital for five days.

Roberto kept playing, hurt or not, for 18 years. He often made remarkable plays, like a catch in Houston that the Astro manager described: **"He took it full flight and hit the wall wide open. It was the best catch I've ever seen."** The last hit of Roberto's career was number 3,000—a figure only a few have reached.

TRUSTWORTHINESS

Roberto Clemente was a courageous ball player.

6 MONTHS IN THE MARINES

In1954 Roberto went to the hospital to visit his dying brother. As Roberto drove home, a speeding, drunken driver crashed into his car. Roberto was glad to be alive, but his spine was permanently injured. From that day on, he played in pain. One year, 1957, the pain was so bad that he thought about quitting baseball. Then he was called up by the United States Marines to serve his country. The six-month rest from baseball seemed to help his back pain.

Roberto learned a lot about back pain in the years following the crash. People often came to him for advice about their own back problems. He helped them by kneading their backs on his basement pool table. They said, **"He has magic in his hands."**

CARING

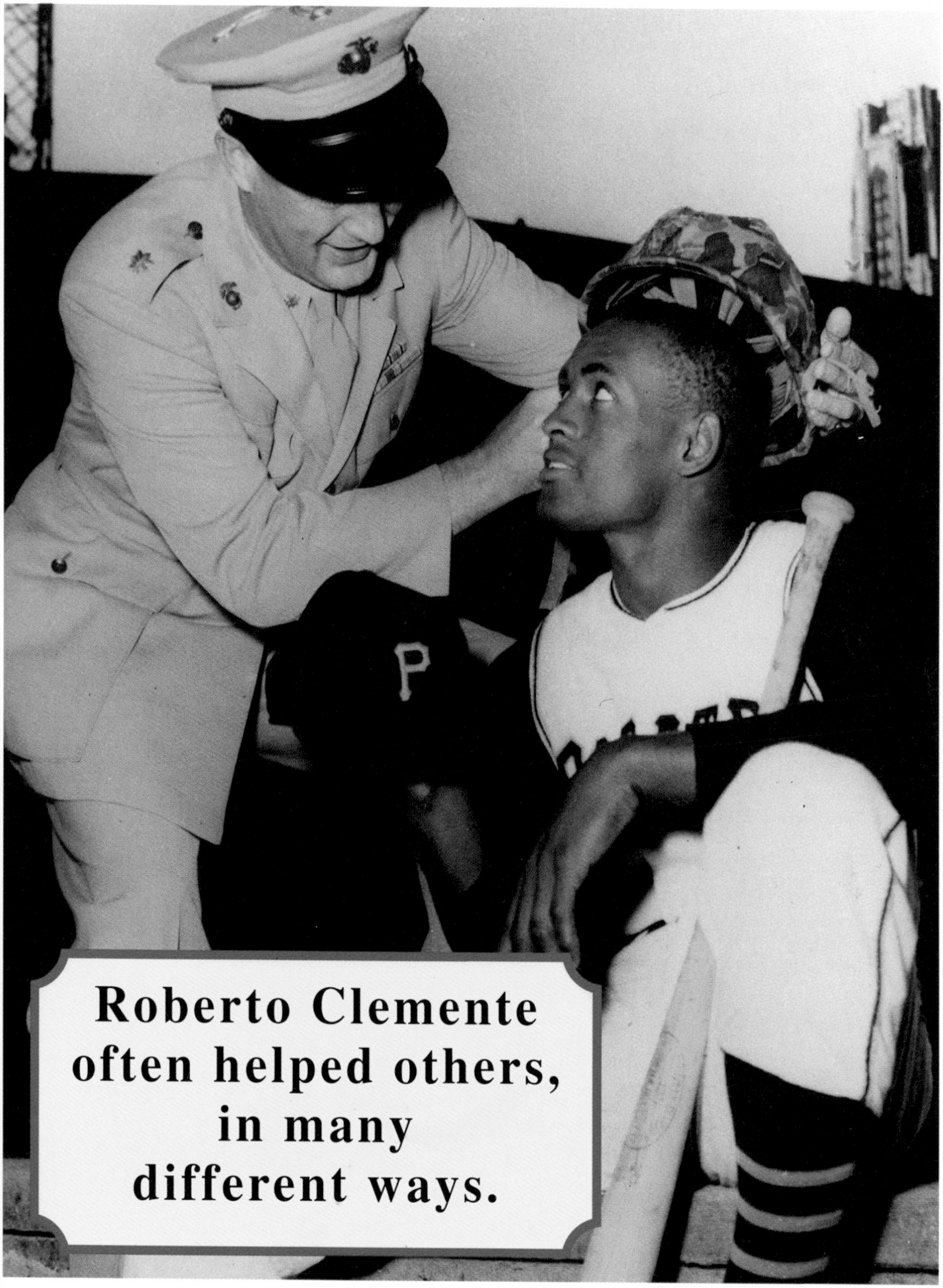

Roberto Clemente often helped others, in many different ways.

7 CHILDREN

Puerto Rico is a small island that has big plantations where sugar cane is grown. Roberto's father worked in the cane fields. He made very little money with which to support his seven children. The family was poor but proud of their heritage.

While playing ball in the United States, Roberto realized that some people were prejudiced against him because he was a poor boy from a poor country who spoke English poorly. Roberto ignored the prejudice. He was proud to be from Puerto Rico. Every year he returned to the island

Roberto Clemente served his country and his community well.

CITIZENSHIP

to play Winter Season ball so his hometown fans could watch him in person. He said, **"A country without idols is nothing. I send out 20,000 autographed pictures a year to the kids. I feel proud when a kid asks me for my autograph. . . I believe we owe something to the people who watch us."**

8 YEARS OLD

At the age of 8, Roberto played baseball his own way. He couldn't afford official equipment, so he made his own. His first bat was a branch from a guava tree, his first mitt a coffee sack, and his first ball was a bunch of rags tied up with string and tape. He practiced throwing and catching all day long and even in bed at night.

As a professional player, Roberto could catch a ball while he was in the air and throw it before landing on his feet. His style was to run fast and throw hard. When he was in right field, **"It was like having four outfielders,"** said a teammate.

Sometimes people compared Roberto to other ball players like Willie Mays. But Roberto was proud of his own style. He said, **"I play only like Roberto Clemente."**

RESPECT FOR OTHERS

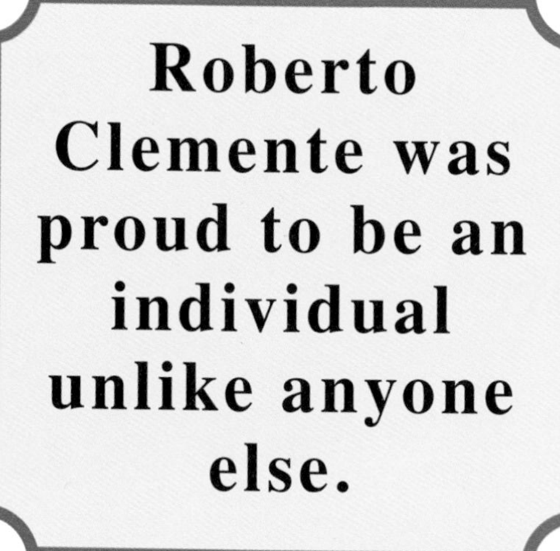

Roberto Clemente was proud to be an individual unlike anyone else.

9 YEARS OLD

At 9, a bike was the thing Roberto wanted most. But his dad told him he had to earn the money himself. So he did. Early every morning he carried a neighbor's empty milk can to the grocery store and carried the full can back again. It took him three years to reach his goal. By the time he was 12, though, he had his bike—and very strong muscles too!

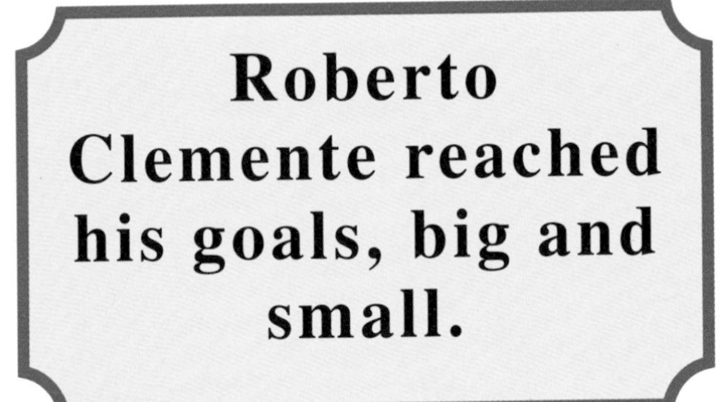

RESPONSIBILITY

10 LETTERS IN EARTHQUAKE

In 1972 a country near Puerto Rico had a terrible earthquake. Roberto Clemente helped collect food and supplies to aid the people of Nicaragua. He even planned to fly

Damage from the earthquake in Nicaragua

RESPONSIBILITY

with the supplies to help pass them out. Soon after take-off, the plane crashed. Everyone on board was killed.

People didn't want to believe that Roberto was dead at such a young age. They stood on the shore, hoping that divers could rescue him. The Governor of Puerto Rico said, **"Our people have lost one of their great glories."** Roberto died doing what he did best—helping others.

SUMMARY

Roberto Clemente's life was too short, but it was filled with goodness. People will always remember his kindness and generosity, his breathtaking efforts and courage on the playing field, and his easy acceptance of others.

From Roberto Clemente we can learn the value of hard work and the importance of sharing good fortune. From Roberto Clemente we can learn what it means to be excellent.

Roberto Clemente's wife and three sons

Roberto Clemente was an American of character.

CITIZENSHIP

The "*Six Pillars of Character*"

Look for the Trustworthiness pillar on the pages about Roberto Clemente. Write what you think trustworthiness means. Some ideas are given below.

Look for the Respect for Others pillar on the pages about Roberto Clemente. Write what you think respect for others means. Some ideas are given below.

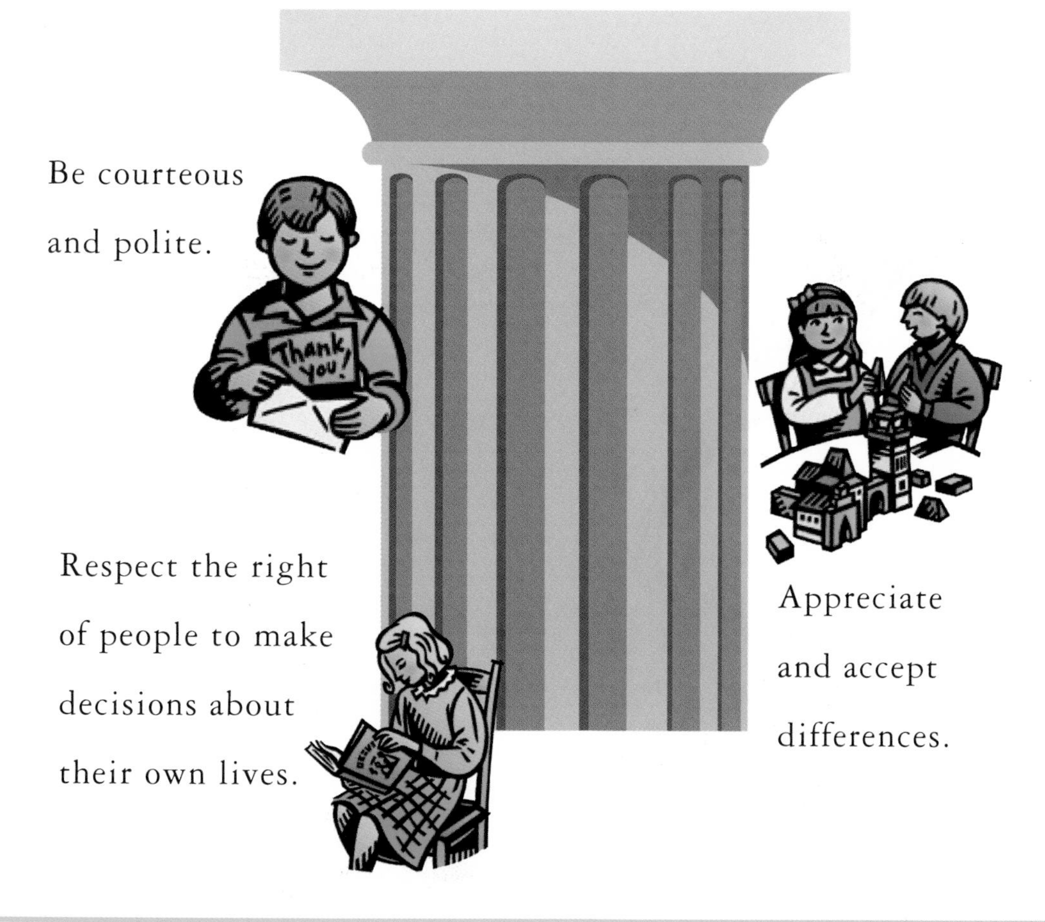

Look for the Responsibility pillar on the pages about Roberto Clemente. Write what you think **responsibility** means. Some ideas are given below.

Look for the Fairness pillar on the pages about Roberto Clemente. Write what you think fairness means. Some ideas are given below.

Look for the Caring pillar on the pages about Roberto Clemente. Write what you think caring means. Some ideas are given below.

CARING

Treat others like you want to be treated.

Show you care about others through kindness, caring, and sharing.

Help others.

Look for the Citizenship pillar on the pages about Roberto Clemente. Write what you think citizenship means. Some ideas are given below.

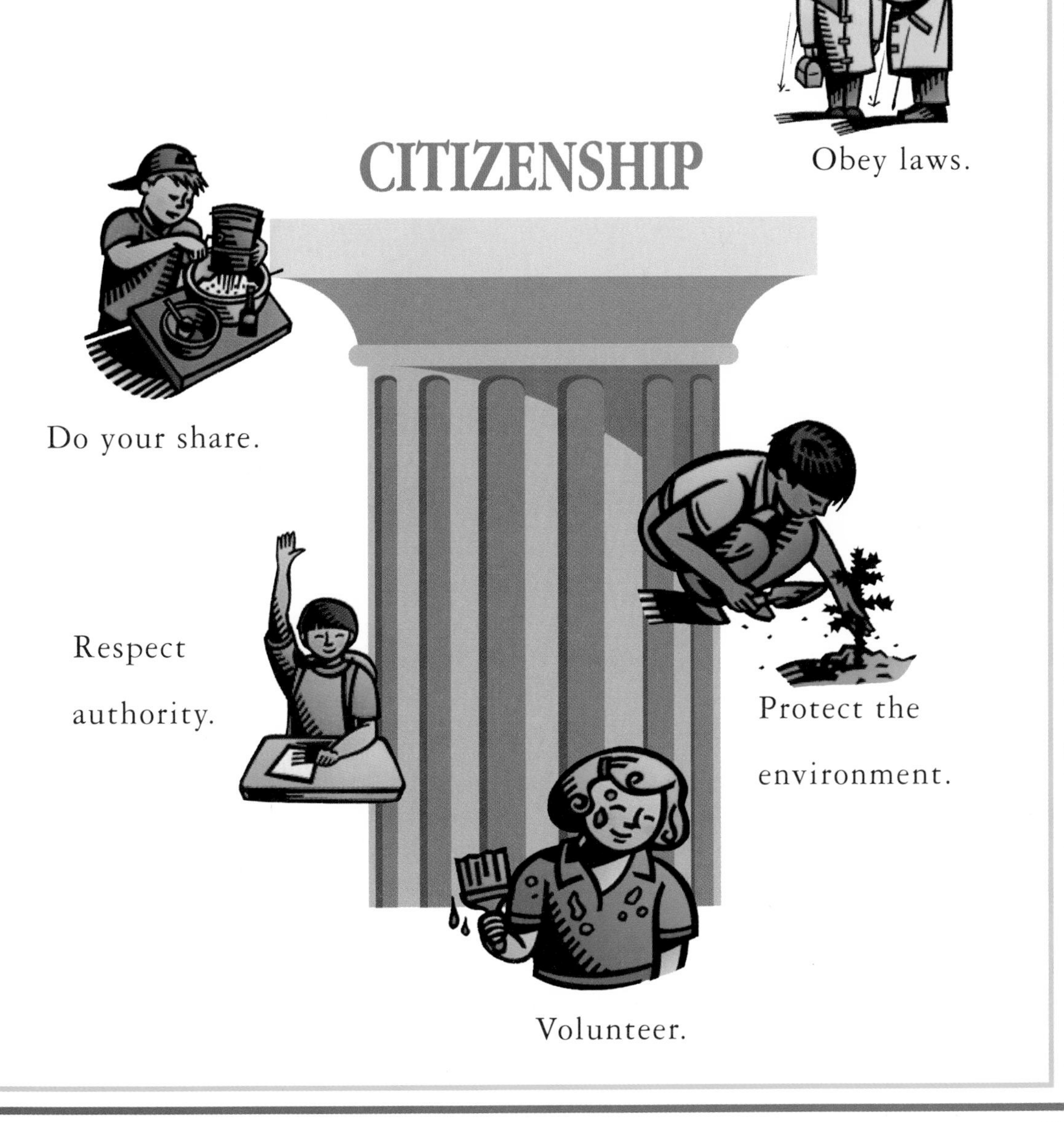

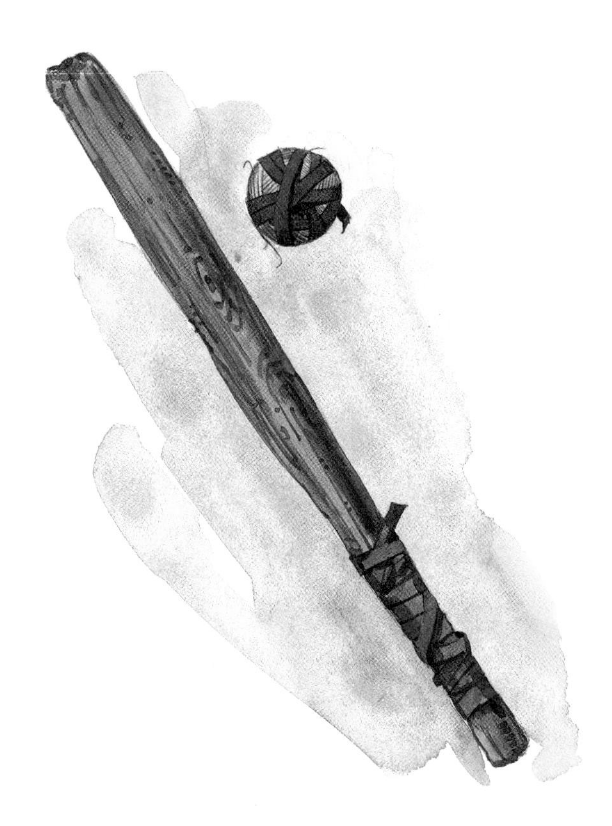

Acknowledgments

The author expresses her special thanks to her first-grade students, who are her keenest editors.

The publisher gratefully acknowledges permission to use the following photographs:

Page i, iii, 3, 4-5, 7, 9, 15, UPI/Bettmann; 11,18,20, AP/WIDE WORLD PHOTOS; 13,21, UPI/Corbis-Bettman.

Illustrations pages ii, 1, 7, 15, 16-17, 19, 28 by John Edens/Creative Freelancers. Illustrations pages 22-27 by Tracy Sabin.